Secretary Bird

by Julie Murray

Abdo Kids Jumbo is an Imprint of Abdo Kids
abdobooks.com

abdobooks.com

Published by Abdo Kids, a division of ABDO, P.O. Box 398166, Minneapolis, Minnesota 55439.

Abdo Kids Jumbo™ is a trademark and logo of Abdo Kids.

Printed in the United States of America, North Mankato, Minnesota.

102024

012025

Photo Credits: Alamy, Getty Images, Minden Pictures, Shutterstock

Production Contributors: Teddy Borth, Jennie Forsberg, Grace Hansen
Design Contributors: Victoria Bates, Candice Keimig

Library of Congress Control Number: 2024936625

Publisher's Cataloging-in-Publication Data

Names: Murray, Julie, author.

Title: Secretary bird / by Julie Murray

Description: Minneapolis, Minnesota : Abdo Kids, 2025 | Series: Unusual animals | Includes online resources and index.

Identifiers: ISBN 9798384903079 (lib. bdg.) | ISBN 9798384903772 (ebook) | ISBN 9798384904120 (Read-to-me ebook)

Subjects: LCSH: Birds--Juvenile literature. | Birds of prey--Juvenile literature. | Flightless birds--Juvenile literature. | Grassland animals--Juvenile literature. | Wildlife--Juvenile literature. | Enigmas--Juvenile literature.

Classification: DDC 598.9--dc23

Table of Contents

Secretary Bird

The secretary bird lives in the grassy plains and **savannas** of Africa. It is closely related to hawks and vultures.

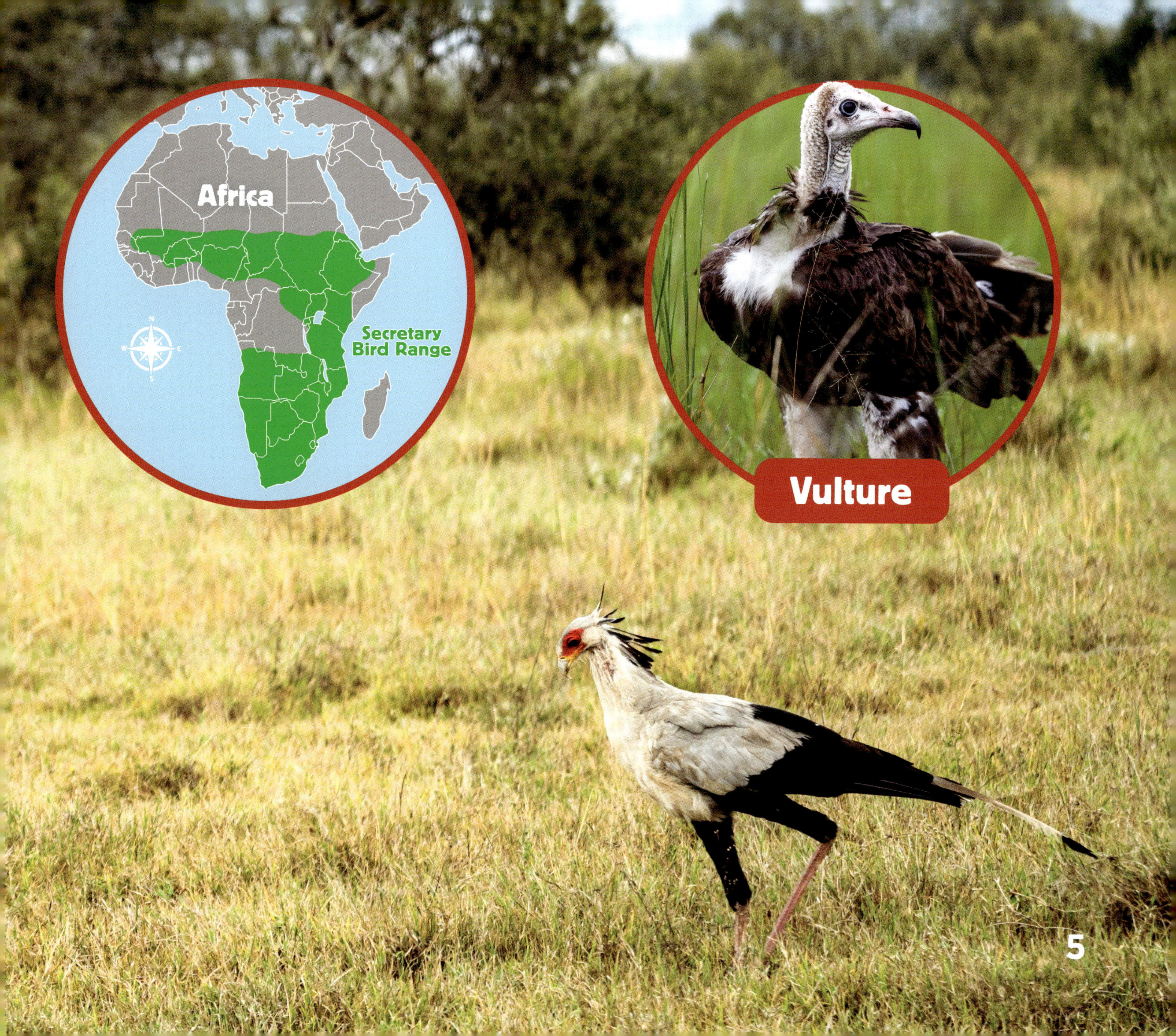
Africa
Secretary
Bird Range
N
W
E
S
Vulture

Secretary birds are unusual! They are only one of two **birds of prey** that hunt for food on foot. They spend their days on the ground. They rest in trees at night.

Secretary birds have whitish-gray body feathers and long, black tail feathers. They have a black **crest** on the back of their head. Their face is bare and orange in color.

Secretary birds have long, thin legs. The bottom halves of their legs do not have feathers. Instead, they are covered in scales that protect them from snake bites!

Food

The secretary bird uses its legs and sharp claws to hunt its **prey**. It feeds on snakes, lizards, and small mammals.

The secretary bird uses quick stomps and kicks to kill its **prey**. It does this with great force. It hunts in pairs or small family groups.

Females lay one to three blue-green eggs at a time. Both males and females **incubate** the eggs. The eggs hatch after about 45 days. Chicks are cared for by their parents for about 80 days.

More Facts

- The secretary bird has a very powerful kick.
- The secretary bird is on the coat of arms of South Africa. It represents protection, rebirth and growth.
- The secretary bird's name is believed to have come from its **crest**. The crest looks like quill pens that male English **secretaries** tucked behind their ears in the 1800s.

Glossary

bird of prey – any bird that feeds on other birds or animals, such as a hawk or vulture.

crest – a tuft of feathers, bone, or fur on an animal's head.

dung – animal poop.

incubate – to keep warm until time to hatch.

prey – an animal that is hunted by other animals for food.

savanna – a flat plain covered with grass that also has scattered trees.

secretary – a person whose job is to write letters, keep records, and manage mail in an office.

wingspan – the distance from the tip of one wing of a bird to the tip of the other.

Index

Visit **abdokids.com** to access crafts, games, videos, and more!